PERSONAL FINANCE MADE EASY

A GUIDE FOR COLLEGE STUDENTS AND YOUNG ADULTS

ADAM VOEGTLI

Contents

1

Introduction

Congratulations on being a college student! This is a time in your life where you have an opportunity to explore your interests, meet new people, and gain valuable skills that can help you achieve your career goals. However, with college life also comes new financial responsibilities, and it's important to start building a solid foundation of personal finance skills early on.

Managing your money well in college can set you up for long-term financial success and stability. It can also help you avoid financial stress and challenges that can impact your academic and personal life. According to a survey conducted by the National Financial Educators Council, only 26% of young adults aged 18-24 could correctly answer basic financial literacy questions. This highlights the importance of financial education and underscores the need for college students to take control of their finances early on.

One of the biggest challenges that college students face is managing their finances. Tuition, housing, books, and other expenses can quickly add up, and without proper financial management, it's easy to fall into debt and financial stress. However, with the right knowledge and strategies, you can learn to manage your money effectively and avoid these pitfalls.

This is where this book comes in. In this guide, we will walk you through the fundamentals of personal finance and provide you with practical strategies to manage your money effectively. Whether you are a freshman just starting out, a sophomore navigating the complexities of student loans, or a senior preparing to enter the workforce, this guide will provide you with the tools you need to make informed financial decisions.

We will start by laying a foundation of financial literacy and goal setting. We believe that financial literacy is the cornerstone of personal finance, and we will provide you with an overview of basic financial terms and concepts that are essential for understanding your money. We will cover topics such as budgeting, managing debt, investing, and saving for the future. We will also discuss the importance of goal setting and how you can use it to create a roadmap for your financial future.

After we have established a solid foundation, we will delve into managing income and expenses. We will explore different ways to find sources of income while in college and discuss how to budget effectively to manage your money. We will also discuss taxes and deductions and provide you with a system for tracking your income. By tracking your income and expenses, you can gain a better understanding of your financial situation and make informed decisions about your spending.

Next, we will discuss saving and investing. We will explore the importance of saving and why it's important to start early. We will also discuss the different types of investment options available and how to develop an investment strategy that works for you. By investing in the stock market or other investment options, you can grow your wealth and achieve your long-term financial goals.

Managing debt is also an essential part of personal finance, and we will provide you with practical strategies for managing and paying off debt. We will discuss different types of debt and how to create a plan for managing and reducing it. We will also provide you with strategies for avoiding debt and maintaining good credit. By managing your debt effectively, you can avoid financial stress and build a strong financial foundation.

Financial planning for the future is also an important topic that we will cover. We will discuss how to create a long-term financial plan that aligns with your personal and professional goals. We will also explore different insurance options and provide guidance on planning for retirement. By planning for the future, you can ensure that you are financially secure and prepared for any unexpected expenses or emergencies.

Finally, we will provide guidance on navigating real-world financial situations. We will discuss how to build credit and manage your credit score. We will also provide you with strategies for making smart financial decisions as a young adult, such as buying a car or renting an apartment. These real-world situations can be overwhelming, but with the right knowledge and strategies, you can make informed decisions and avoid financial mistakes that can impact your long-term financial goals.

In conclusion, we hope that this guide will empower you to take control of your personal finances and achieve your long-term financial goals. By following the strategies outlined in this book, you can build a solid financial foundation that will set you up for success in college and beyond. Remember, managing your money effectively is not just about achieving financial stability, but also about creating a sense of freedom and control in your life. With the right knowledge and tools, you can make informed financial decisions and achieve your personal and professional goals.

We understand that personal finance can be a complex and overwhelming topic, especially for college students who are juggling academic and personal responsibilities. However, with this guide, we hope to provide you with a clear and concise roadmap for managing your finances effectively. We will walk you through the steps needed to create a budget, manage your income and expenses, save and invest for the future, manage debt, and plan for the future. We will also provide you with real-world examples and practical strategies for making informed financial decisions as a young adult.

Finally, we want to remind you that personal finance is not just about numbers and budgets, it's about your values, goals, and aspirations. By taking control of your finances and achieving your financial goals, you can create a sense of freedom and control in your life. We wish you the best of luck on your personal finance journey and hope that this guide will provide you with the knowledge and tools you need to achieve financial success and stability.

2

WHAT PERSONAL FINANCE MEANS TO A STUDENT

Managing personal finances is an essential skill for college students, but it can be challenging to navigate the complex world of personal finance. In this chapter, we will provide you with a comprehensive overview of personal finance and its importance. We will discuss the fundamentals of personal finance, including budgeting, saving, investing, and managing debt. We will also provide guidance on how to develop good financial habits, overcome financial barriers, and protect yourself from financial scams and fraud.

A. Personal finance impacts all areas of your life

Personal finance impacts every aspect of your life, from your ability to pay for college to your ability to buy a car, a house, or other major purchases. Good financial management can help you achieve your financial goals, reduce financial stress, and provide financial security and independence. Poor financial management, on the other hand, can lead to debt, financial stress, and a lack of financial security.

B. The importance of financial independence

Financial independence is the ability to support yourself and your family without relying on others for financial assistance. Financial independence provides you with the freedom and flexibility to pursue your goals and dreams, whether that means starting a business, traveling, or saving for retirement.

C. The consequences of poor financial management

Poor financial management can have serious consequences, including debt, bankruptcy, and a lack of financial security. It can also lead to missed opportunities, such as being unable to take advantage of a good investment opportunity or being unable to pursue a career you are passionate about.

II. Building a Foundation

A. Understanding basic financial terms and concepts

To manage your personal finances effectively, you need to understand basic financial terms and concepts such as budgeting, saving, investing, and managing debt. These concepts are essential for building a strong financial foundation and achieving your financial goals.

B. Setting financial goals

Setting financial goals is essential for managing your personal finances effectively. Financial goals provide you with a clear direction and motivation to achieve your financial aspirations. Your financial goals should be specific, measurable, achievable, relevant, and time-bound (SMART).

C. Creating a budget

Creating a budget is an essential part of managing your personal finances effectively. A budget helps you track your income and expenses, identify areas where you can save money, and allocate resources towards your financial goals. To create a budget, you should start by identifying your income sources and expenses, prioritizing your spending, and monitoring your budget regularly.

D. Assessing your financial situation

Before you can create a budget or set financial goals, you need to assess your current financial situation. This includes identifying your income sources, expenses, assets, and debts. You should also calculate your net worth and debt-to-income ratio, which can help you understand your overall financial health.

For example, let's say you are considering buying a car. By assessing your financial situation and understanding how much you can afford to spend, you can make an informed decision about whether to buy a car and how much to spend.

E. Prioritizing your spending

When creating a budget, it's important to prioritize your spending to ensure that your essential expenses are covered first. Essential expenses include things like housing, food, transportation, and healthcare. Discretionary expenses, such as entertainment and travel, should be considered after essential expenses are accounted for.

For example, let's say you are trying to save money. By prioritizing your spending and focusing on essential expenses such as housing, food, and transportation, you can reduce your expenses and save more money.

F. Developing good financial habits

Developing good financial habits is essential for managing your personal finances effectively. Good financial habits include things like saving regularly, tracking your expenses, and avoiding impulse purchases. By developing good financial habits, you can make consistent progress towards your financial goals.

For example, let's say you want to save money for a down payment on a house. By developing good financial habits and saving regularly, you can make consistent progress towards your savings goal.

G. Overcoming financial barriers

There are many financial barriers that can make it difficult to manage your personal finances effectively. These barriers may include things like low income, high expenses, or a lack of financial education. To overcome these barriers, you may need to seek guidance from financial professionals, develop a support network, and educate yourself on personal finance topics.

For example, let's say you are struggling with debt and don't know where to turn. By seeking guidance from a financial professional and connecting with other people who are facing similar challenges, you can gain the support and resources needed to overcome your financial stress.

H. Understanding your money mindset

Your money mindset refers to your beliefs and attitudes about money. These beliefs and attitudes can have a significant impact on your financial decisions and behaviors. By understanding your money mindset, you can identify any limiting beliefs or negative attitudes that may be holding you back from achieving your financial goals.

For example, let's say you have a limiting belief that you will never be able to save enough money to buy a house. By identifying this belief and challenging it, you can start to change your mindset and make progress towards your goal.

I. Developing financial literacy

Financial literacy refers to your knowledge and understanding of personal finance concepts and principles. Developing financial literacy is essential for managing your personal finances effectively. It can help you make informed financial decisions, avoid common financial pitfalls, and achieve your financial goals.

For example, let's say you are considering investing in the stock market. By developing financial literacy and understanding the risks and rewards associated with investing, you can make informed decisions about how to invest your money.

III. Managing Your Money

A. Managing debt

Managing debt is an essential part of managing your personal finances effectively. To manage your debt, you should prioritize high-interest debts first, make regular payments, and avoid taking on new debt.

For example, let's say you have credit card debt with a high-interest rate. By prioritizing this debt first and making regular payments, you can reduce your overall debt and save money on interest charges.

B. Building credit

Building credit is essential for obtaining credit, loans, and other financial products. To build your credit, you should make on-time payments, keep your credit utilization low, and avoid opening too many new accounts.

For example, let's say you want to apply for a car loan. By building your credit score and maintaining a good credit history, you can increase your chances of being approved and receiving favorable terms.

C. Saving money

Saving money is an essential part of managing your personal finances effectively. To save money, you should develop a savings plan, set specific savings goals, and make regular contributions to your savings.

For example, let's say you want to save money for a vacation. By developing a savings plan and setting specific savings goals, you can save money consistently and achieve your goal.

D. Developing a savings plan

Developing a savings plan involves identifying your savings goals, creating a budget, and setting aside a specific amount of money for savings each month. A savings plan can help you stay focused and motivated, and can help you achieve your financial goals over time.

For example, let's say you want to save money for a down payment on a house. By developing a savings plan and setting aside a specific amount of money each month, you can make steady progress towards your goal.

E. Building an emergency fund

Building an emergency fund is essential for managing your personal finances effectively. An emergency fund is a savings account that is designed to cover unexpected expenses, such as car repairs or medical bills. To build an emergency fund, you should set aside a specific amount of money each month and avoid touching the funds unless it is necessary.

For example, let's say you have unexpected car repairs. By having an emergency fund, you can cover the expense without having to take on debt or disrupt your other financial goals.

F. Understanding the time value of money

The time value of money is a fundamental concept in personal finance. It refers to the idea that money available today is worth more than the same amount of money available in the future. This is due to the potential for money to earn interest over time.

For example, let's say you are considering two investment options. Option A offers a 5% return over five years, while option B offers a 7% return over seven years. By understanding the time value of money, you can calculate the present value of each option and choose the one that offers the highest return.

G. Understanding investment options

Investing can be a powerful tool for building wealth over time. There are many different types of investments, including stocks, bonds, mutual funds, and real estate. Each type of investment has its own risks and rewards, and it's important to understand these before investing your money.

For example, let's say you are considering investing in mutual funds. By understanding the risks and rewards associated with mutual funds, you can make an informed decision about how to invest your money.

H. Balancing short-term and long-term goals

Balancing short-term and long-term financial goals can be a challenge, especially for college students who may have competing priorities. To balance these goals, you should prioritize your financial goals, set realistic timelines, and manage competing demands.

For example, let's say you want to save money for a vacation, but you also want to save money for retirement. By prioritizing your financial goals and setting realistic timelines, you can make progress towards both goals over time.

IV. Protecting Your Finances

A. Identifying financial scams and fraud

Financial scams and fraud can have a devastating impact on your personal finances. To protect yourself from financial scams and fraud, you should be aware of common scams, such as phishing and identity theft, and take steps to protect your personal information.

For example, let's say you receive an email from someone claiming to be from your bank and asking for your account information. By identifying the email as a phishing scam and taking appropriate action, such as reporting it to your bank, you can avoid becoming a victim of financial fraud.

B. Protecting your identity

Identity theft is a serious threat to your personal finances. To protect your identity, you should be careful about sharing your personal information, monitor your credit report regularly, and take steps to protect your online accounts and devices.

For example, let's say you receive a suspicious email asking for your personal information. By taking steps to protect your identity, such as not responding to the email and contacting your bank to report the suspicious activity, you can avoid becoming a victim of identity theft.

C. Managing financial stress

Financial stress can have a significant impact on your mental and physical health, and can make it difficult to manage your finances effectively. To manage financial stress, you should identify the sources of stress, develop coping strategies, and seek support from others.

For example, let's say you are experiencing financial stress due to debt. By seeking support from friends or family, talking to a financial advisor, and developing a debt repayment plan, you can reduce your stress and make progress towards your financial goals.

D. Understanding financial decision-making biases

Financial decision-making biases can affect your ability to make sound financial decisions. By understanding common biases, such as loss aversion and confirmation bias, you can make more rational financial decisions.

For example, let's say you are considering investing in a stock that has recently experienced a significant decline in value. By recognizing your own loss aversion bias and seeking advice from a financial advisor, you can make a more informed decision about whether to invest in the stock.

E. Understanding insurance

Insurance is a tool for managing risk and protecting your finances from unexpected events, such as accidents or illnesses. To understand insurance, you should understand the different types of insurance, such as health insurance, car insurance, and life insurance, and assess your own insurance needs.

For example, let's say you are considering purchasing a car. By understanding your insurance needs and shopping around for car insurance quotes, you can find a policy that provides the coverage you need at an affordable price.

F. Estate planning

Estate planning is the process of making decisions about what happens to your assets and property after you die. Estate planning can help ensure that your wishes are carried out, and can also help reduce estate taxes and avoid probate.

For example, let's say you have a significant amount of assets and property. By developing an estate plan and working with an estate planning attorney, you can ensure that your assets and property are distributed according to your wishes and minimize estate taxes.

Conclusion

Managing personal finances can be challenging, but it's an essential skill for college students. By building a strong financial foundation, managing your money effectively, and protecting your finances, you can achieve your financial goals and enjoy greater financial security and independence. The key to success is to educate yourself, develop good financial habits, and seek guidance and support when needed. By doing so, you can take control of your finances and achieve your financial aspirations.

In conclusion, personal finance is a critical aspect of daily life that can impact your financial stability and overall well-being. As a college student, it's important to start taking steps to manage your personal finances effectively, as this can set the foundation for your future financial success. By understanding basic financial terms and concepts, setting financial goals, creating a budget, managing your debt, building credit, and saving money, you can develop good financial habits and make consistent progress towards your financial goals. Protecting your finances from scams, identity theft, and other financial stressors is also essential for achieving financial security.

While managing personal finances can be a challenging and sometimes overwhelming process, there are many resources and tools available to help you along the way. You can seek guidance and support from financial professionals, such as financial advisors, accountants, or tax professionals, and you can also tap into the vast array of online resources available to help you learn more about personal finance. Ultimately, the key to managing personal finances effectively is to stay informed, stay focused on your financial goals, and remain committed to developing good financial habits.

By taking control of your personal finances, you can achieve financial security and independence, which can have a significant impact on your overall quality of life. You can reduce your financial stress and anxiety, increase your confidence and peace of mind, and achieve your financial aspirations. So, start today by taking the first step towards managing your personal finances effectively.

3

ALL ABOUT INCOME

A. Finding sources of income while in college

As a college student, finding sources of income can be challenging, but it's an essential part of managing your personal finances effectively. There are several ways you can earn money while in college, such as getting a part-time job, working as a tutor or research assistant, or freelancing online.

For example, let's say you are looking for a part-time job. By researching job openings on campus or in your local area, you can find opportunities that fit your schedule and pay a reasonable wage. You can also consider freelancing online, such as through platforms like Fiverr or Upwork, to earn extra money on your own time.

B. Understanding taxes and deductions

Understanding taxes and deductions is essential for managing your income effectively. Taxes are a percentage of your income that you are required to pay to the government, while deductions are expenses that can reduce your taxable income. By understanding taxes and deductions, you can ensure that you are paying the appropriate amount of taxes and taking advantage of any available deductions.

For example, let's say you have a part-time job and are earning income. By understanding how much of your income is subject to taxes, you can estimate how much you will owe in taxes and plan accordingly. You can also look for deductions, such as education expenses or student loan interest, to reduce your taxable income.

C. Developing a system for tracking income

Developing a system for tracking your income is essential for managing your personal finances effectively. By tracking your income, you can ensure that you are getting paid the correct amount, monitor your progress towards your financial goals, and identify areas where you can make improvements.

For example, let's say you are working as a freelance writer and earning income from several clients. By developing a system for tracking your income, such as using a spreadsheet or a financial tracking app, you can keep track of how much you are earning from each client and ensure that you are paid the correct amount.

D. Maximizing your income

Maximizing your income is essential for achieving your financial goals and managing your personal finances effectively. There are several ways you can maximize your income, such as negotiating your salary, asking for a raise, or seeking out higher-paying job opportunities.

For example, let's say you are working at a part-time job and want to increase your income. By negotiating your salary or asking for a raise, you can potentially earn more money without having to find a new job. You can also seek out higher-paying job opportunities, such as internships or part-time positions in your field of study, to maximize your income.

E. Managing irregular income

Managing irregular income can be challenging, but it's an essential part of managing your personal finances effectively. Irregular income can come from sources like freelancing, seasonal work, or commissions, and can vary in amount from month to month. To manage irregular income, you should develop a budget that takes into account your average income and expenses, save money during high-income months, and prioritize essential expenses during low-income months.

For example, let's say you are earning income from freelancing and your income varies from month to month. By developing a budget that takes into account your average income and expenses, you can ensure that you are able to cover your essential expenses even during low-income months. You can also save money during high-income months to help cover expenses during low-income months.

F. Evaluating income opportunities

Evaluating income opportunities is essential for managing your personal finances effectively. Before accepting a job or taking on a new income opportunity, you should consider factors such as the amount of income, the required time commitment, and the potential for career advancement.

For example, let's say you are considering a part-time job offer that pays minimum wage but offers opportunities for advancement. By evaluating the income opportunity, you can determine whether it is worth the time commitment and whether the potential for career advancement outweighs the lower wage.

G. Budgeting for fixed and variable expenses

Budgeting for fixed and variable expenses is essential for managing your personal finances effectively. Fixed expenses, such as rent or a car payment, are expenses that stay the same from month to month, while variable expenses, such as groceries or entertainment, can vary in amount from month to month. To budget for fixed and variable expenses, you should identify your essential expenses, create a budget that takes into account your income and expenses, and track your spending to ensure that you are staying within your budget.

For example, let's say you are a college student with a part-time job and have both fixed expenses, such as rent and utilities, and variable expenses, such as groceries and entertainment. By identifying your essential expenses, creating a budget that takes into account your income and expenses, and tracking your spending, you can ensure that you are able to cover your essential expenses and save money for your financial goals.

H. Creating a debt repayment plan

Creating a debt repayment plan is essential for managing your personal finances effectively, especially if you have student loans or credit card debt. To create a debt repayment plan, you should identify your debts, create a budget that takes into account your debt payments, and prioritize your debt repayment based on interest rates and balances.

For example, let's say you have student loans and credit card debt. By identifying your debts, creating a budget that takes into account your debt payments, and prioritizing your debt repayment based on interest rates and balances, you can make progress towards paying off your debt and achieving your financial goals.

I. Understanding credit scores and reports

Understanding credit scores and reports is essential for managing your personal finances effectively. Your credit score is a number that reflects your creditworthiness, while your credit report is a summary of your credit history. By understanding your credit score and report, you can improve your creditworthiness, access credit when you need it, and avoid costly mistakes that can damage your credit.

For example, let's say you are considering applying for a credit card. By understanding your credit score and report, you can ensure that you are able to access credit and get the best possible interest rate. You can also take steps to improve your credit score, such as paying bills on time and keeping credit card balances low.

J. Building credit

Building credit is essential for managing your personal finances effectively. Your credit history is a reflection of your creditworthiness, and having good credit can help you access credit when you need it, such as when you apply for a loan or a credit card. To build credit, you should make payments on time, keep credit card balances low, and avoid opening too many new credit accounts.

For example, let's say you are a college student and want to build your credit history. By making payments on time, keeping credit card balances low, and avoiding opening too many new credit accounts, you can build a good credit history and increase your creditworthiness.

K. Negotiating job offers and salaries

Negotiating job offers and salaries is an essential part of managing your income effectively. By negotiating, you can potentially earn more money and improve your overall financial situation. To negotiate effectively, you should research the job market, understand your own worth, and be prepared to make a strong case for your desired salary or benefits.

For example, let's say you are offered a job but the starting salary is lower than you were hoping for. By researching the job market, understanding your own worth, and making a strong case for your desired salary or benefits, you may be able to negotiate a higher salary or better benefits.

L. Applying for financial aid and scholarships

Applying for financial aid and scholarships is an important part of managing your income effectively, especially if you are paying for college on your own. Financial aid and scholarships can help you cover the cost of tuition, fees, and other expenses, reducing the amount of money you need to earn or borrow.

For example, let's say you are a college student and need help paying for tuition. By applying for financial aid and scholarships, you may be able to cover the cost of tuition and reduce the amount of money you need to earn or borrow.

M. Managing multiple sources of income

Managing multiple sources of income can be challenging, but it's an important part of managing your income effectively. If you have multiple sources of income, such as a part-time job and freelance work, you will need to keep track of all your earnings, expenses, and tax obligations.

For example, let's say you have a part-time job and do freelance work on the side. By keeping track of all your earnings, expenses, and tax obligations, you can ensure that you are paid the correct amount and are in compliance with all tax laws.

N. Investing income for long-term growth

Investing income for long-term growth is an important part of managing your income effectively. If you have extra income that you don't need for immediate expenses, you can invest it to potentially earn a higher return over time.

For example, let's say you have a part-time job and are earning extra income that you don't need for immediate expenses. By investing that income in a diversified portfolio of stocks, bonds, and other assets, you may be able to earn a higher return over time and build wealth for the future.

O. Setting up a retirement account

Setting up a retirement account is an important part of managing your income effectively, especially if you are starting to earn income while in college. A retirement account, such as an Individual Retirement Account (IRA) or a 401(k), can help you save for retirement and potentially earn a higher return on your investment over time.

For example, let's say you have a part-time job and are starting to earn income. By setting up an IRA or a 401(k), you can start saving for retirement and potentially earn a higher return on your investment over time.

P. Understanding the gig economy

Understanding the gig economy is important for managing your income effectively, as more and more people are turning to freelance work and other non-traditional income sources. By understanding the gig economy, you can identify new income opportunities, learn about the potential risks and benefits of gig work, and stay informed about changes in the job market.

For example, let's say you are a college student and want to earn extra income through freelance work. By understanding the gig economy, you can learn about different platforms and services that connect freelancers with clients, identify the best opportunities for your skills and experience, and stay informed about changes in the job market.

Q. Developing a side hustle

Developing a side hustle is a great way to earn extra income and potentially build a new career or business. A side hustle can be any type of work or project that you do outside of your regular job or school commitments.

For example, let's say you are a college student and have a passion for writing. By developing a side hustle as a freelance writer or starting a blog, you can earn extra income and potentially build a career in writing.

R. Managing income during the summer

Managing income during the summer is an important part of managing your personal finances effectively, especially if you are a college student with seasonal work or other summer employment. By managing your income effectively during the summer, you can cover your expenses, save for your financial goals, and prepare for the coming academic year.

For example, let's say you are a college student with a summer job. By managing your income effectively, you can ensure that you have enough money to cover your expenses during the summer, save for your financial goals, and prepare for the coming academic year.

S. Understanding financial aid packages

Understanding financial aid packages is important for managing your income effectively, especially if you are a college student who is relying on financial aid to pay for tuition and other expenses. Financial aid packages can include grants, scholarships, loans, and work-study programs, and understanding the terms and conditions of your aid package is essential for managing your finances effectively.

For example, let's say you are a college student who has been offered a financial aid package that includes both grants and loans. By understanding the terms and conditions of your aid package, you can ensure that you are able to cover your expenses and minimize your debt.

T. Managing income during internships

Managing income during internships is important for managing your personal finances effectively, especially if you are a college student who is relying on income from internships to cover expenses. By managing your income effectively during internships, you can cover your expenses, save for your financial goals, and gain valuable work experience.

For example, let's say you are a college student who is completing an unpaid internship. By managing your income effectively, you can ensure that you have enough money to cover your expenses during the internship, save for your financial goals, and gain valuable work experience that can help you build your career.

U. Understanding and managing taxes on side income

Understanding and managing taxes on side income is important for managing your personal finances effectively, especially if you are earning income from freelance work or other non-traditional sources. By understanding how taxes work on side income, you can ensure that you are paying the correct amount of taxes and avoiding potential penalties or fines.

For example, let's say you are a college student who is earning income from freelance writing. By understanding how taxes work on side income, you can ensure that you are paying the correct amount of taxes and keeping accurate records of your income and expenses.

Conclusion

Managing income is an essential part of managing your personal finances effectively. By finding sources of income while in college, understanding taxes and deductions, developing a system for tracking income, maximizing your income, managing irregular income, evaluating income opportunities, budgeting for fixed and variable expenses, creating a debt repayment plan, understanding credit scores and reports, and building credit, you can achieve financial security and independence. The key to success is to stay informed, develop good financial habits, and seek guidance and support when needed. By doing so, you can take control of your personal finances and achieve your financial aspirations.

4

TAKING EXPENSES INTO CONSIDERATION

Managing expenses is an essential part of personal finance, and it's particularly important for college students who are learning to live independently and manage their own finances. In this chapter, we will discuss how to identify fixed and variable expenses, create a plan for managing expenses, and strategies for reducing expenses.

A. Identifying fixed and variable expenses

The first step in managing expenses is to identify your fixed and variable expenses. Fixed expenses are expenses that stay the same from month to month, such as rent, car payments, and insurance premiums. Variable expenses are expenses that can vary in amount from month to month, such as groceries, entertainment, and travel.

To identify your fixed and variable expenses, you should create a list of all your regular expenses, including bills, groceries, transportation, and other expenses. This will give you a clear understanding of your spending habits and help you create a budget that takes into account your income and expenses.

B. Creating a plan for managing expenses

Once you have identified your fixed and variable expenses, you should create a plan for managing your expenses. This plan should take into account your income, expenses, and financial goals, and should be flexible enough to adapt to changes in your income or expenses.

To create a plan for managing expenses, you should start by creating a budget that includes all your income and expenses, including your fixed and variable expenses. You should also set financial goals, such as saving for a down payment on a home or paying off student loans, and allocate funds towards achieving these goals.

C. Strategies for reducing expenses

Reducing expenses is an important part of managing your personal finances effectively, especially if you are on a limited budget. Here are some strategies for reducing expenses:

Cut back on unnecessary expenses

One of the easiest ways to reduce expenses is to cut back on unnecessary expenses. This may include eating out less frequently, canceling subscriptions or memberships that you don't use, or finding cheaper alternatives for entertainment and leisure activities.

Shop for deals and discounts

Another way to reduce expenses is to shop for deals and discounts. This may include shopping for groceries at discount stores, using coupons or promo codes when shopping online, or taking advantage of student discounts at local businesses.

Consider sharing expenses

Sharing expenses with roommates or friends is another way to reduce expenses. This may include splitting the cost of rent, utilities, or groceries, or sharing transportation costs by carpooling or using public transportation.

Negotiate bills and contracts

Negotiating bills and contracts is another way to reduce expenses. This may include negotiating a lower interest rate on a credit card, negotiating a lower rate for your cell phone or internet service, or negotiating a lower price for a car or home insurance policy.

By identifying fixed and variable expenses, creating a plan for managing expenses, and implementing strategies for reducing expenses, you can effectively manage your personal finances and achieve your financial goals. The key is to stay informed, stay flexible, and be proactive in managing your expenses.

D. Managing credit card debt

Managing credit card debt is an important part of managing expenses, particularly for college students who may be using credit cards to cover expenses while in school. Credit card debt can be a major source of financial stress, and it can also impact your credit score, making it harder to secure loans or other forms of credit in the future.

To manage credit card debt effectively, you should start by reviewing your credit card statements and identifying your outstanding balances and interest rates. You should then create a plan for paying off your credit card debt, prioritizing your balances based on interest rates and minimum payments.

Here are some strategies for managing credit card debt:

Pay more than the minimum payment

Paying more than the minimum payment is one of the most effective ways to manage credit card debt. By paying more than the minimum payment, you can reduce the amount of interest that accrues and pay off your debt more quickly.

Consider a balance transfer

A balance transfer can be a good option for managing credit card debt, particularly if you have high-interest balances on multiple cards. A balance transfer allows you to transfer your balances to a single credit card with a lower interest rate, potentially saving you money on interest and making it easier to manage your payments.

Avoid using credit cards for unnecessary expenses

To avoid adding to your credit card debt, you should avoid using credit cards for unnecessary expenses. This may include cutting back on entertainment or leisure expenses, finding cheaper alternatives for necessities like groceries and transportation, and avoiding impulse purchases.

E. Managing student loans

Managing student loans is another important part of managing expenses for college students. Student loans can be a major source of debt and financial stress, and it's important to have a plan for paying off your loans while also managing your other expenses.

To manage student loans effectively, you should start by reviewing your loan statements and identifying your outstanding balances, interest rates, and payment schedules. You should then create a plan for paying off your loans, taking into account your income, expenses, and financial goals.

Here are some strategies for managing student loans:

Make payments on time

Making payments on time is important for managing student loans, as late payments can result in fees, penalties, and damage to your credit score. To ensure that you make payments on time, you may want to set up automatic payments or create reminders for yourself.

Consider refinancing or consolidation

Refinancing or consolidating your student loans can be a good option for managing your debt, particularly if you have multiple loans with different interest rates and payment schedules. Refinancing or consolidation can potentially lower your interest rates and simplify your payments, making it easier to manage your debt.

Consider income-driven repayment plans

Income-driven repayment plans can be a good option for managing student loans, particularly if you have a low income or are struggling to make your payments. Income-driven repayment plans adjust your payments based on your income, potentially reducing your monthly payments and making it easier to manage your debt.

By managing credit card debt and student loans effectively, college students can reduce their financial stress and achieve their financial goals more quickly. The key is to stay informed, create a plan for paying off your debt, and take action to reduce your expenses and increase your income. By doing so, you can achieve financial security and independence, reduce financial stress, and achieve your financial aspirations.

F. Managing housing and utilities expenses

Managing housing and utilities expenses is a major part of managing expenses for college students, particularly if you are living off-campus or in an apartment. These expenses can add up quickly, but there are strategies you can use to manage them effectively.

To manage housing and utilities expenses effectively, you should start by reviewing your lease or rental agreement and identifying your monthly rent and utility costs. You should then create a plan for managing these expenses, taking into account your income, expenses, and financial goals.

Here are some strategies for managing housing and utilities expenses:

Find affordable housing

Finding affordable housing is one of the most effective ways to manage housing expenses. This may include finding roommates to split the cost of rent, finding an apartment in a less expensive neighborhood, or looking for housing options that offer student discounts.

Reduce utility costs

Reducing your utility costs is another way to manage housing expenses. This may include taking steps to conserve energy, such as turning off lights and unplugging electronics when not in use, or installing energy-efficient appliances and light bulbs.

Negotiate rent or utility costs

Negotiating your rent or utility costs is another way to manage housing expenses. This may include negotiating a lower rent with your landlord, negotiating a lower rate for your internet or cable service, or finding ways to reduce your water or electricity bills.

G. Managing transportation expenses

Managing transportation expenses is another important part of managing expenses for college students, particularly if you are commuting to campus or to work. Transportation expenses can include gas, car payments, insurance, and public transportation costs.

To manage transportation expenses effectively, you should start by reviewing your transportation costs and identifying areas where you can reduce your expenses. You should then create a plan for managing these expenses, taking into account your income, expenses, and financial goals.

Here are some strategies for managing transportation expenses:

Use public transportation

Using public transportation is one of the most effective ways to manage transportation expenses. This may include taking the bus, subway, or train to campus or work, or using a bike or scooter to get around.

Carpool or share rides

Carpooling or sharing rides is another way to manage transportation expenses. This may include sharing a ride with a classmate or coworker, or using a ride-sharing service like Uber or Lyft to split the cost of transportation.

Find affordable car insurance

Finding affordable car insurance is another way to manage transportation expenses. This may include shopping around for the best rates, or taking steps to reduce your insurance premiums, such as maintaining a safe driving record or installing anti-theft devices in your car.

By managing housing and utilities expenses and transportation expenses effectively, college students can reduce their financial stress and achieve their financial goals more quickly. The key is to stay informed, create a plan for managing your expenses, and take action to reduce your expenses and increase your income. By doing so, you can achieve financial security and independence, reduce financial stress, and achieve your financial aspirations.

H. Managing healthcare expenses

Managing healthcare expenses is an important part of managing expenses for college students, particularly if you are not covered by a parent's health insurance plan or a school-sponsored plan. Healthcare expenses can include insurance premiums, co-payments, deductibles, and out-of-pocket expenses.

To manage healthcare expenses effectively, you should start by reviewing your healthcare costs and identifying your insurance coverage and out-of-pocket expenses. You should then create a plan for managing these expenses, taking into account your income, expenses, and financial goals.

Here are some strategies for managing healthcare expenses:

Find affordable health insurance

Finding affordable health insurance is one of the most effective ways to manage healthcare expenses. This may include finding an insurance plan that offers low premiums and deductibles, or finding a plan that offers coverage for preventive care and other essential services.

Use preventive care services

Using preventive care services is another way to manage healthcare expenses. Preventive care services can help you stay healthy and catch potential health problems before they become more serious, potentially reducing your overall healthcare costs.

Find affordable prescription medications

Finding affordable prescription medications is another way to manage healthcare expenses. This may include using a generic version of a medication, finding prescription discount programs, or shopping around for the best prices.

I. Managing unexpected expenses

Managing unexpected expenses is an important part of managing expenses for college students, particularly if you are on a limited budget. Unexpected expenses can include car repairs, medical bills, or other unforeseen events that can impact your finances.

To manage unexpected expenses effectively, you should create an emergency fund that can help you cover unexpected expenses without derailing your financial goals. An emergency fund should ideally cover at least three to six months of your living expenses.

Here are some strategies for managing unexpected expenses:

Start an emergency fund

Starting an emergency fund is one of the most effective ways to manage unexpected expenses. An emergency fund can help you cover unexpected expenses without derailing your financial goals, and it can also provide a sense of financial security and peace of mind.

Avoid using credit cards for emergency expenses

To avoid adding to your debt, you should avoid using credit cards for emergency expenses. Instead, you should use your emergency fund or explore other options for covering unexpected expenses, such as borrowing from family or friends.

Consider insurance

Insurance can be a good option for managing unexpected expenses, particularly if you have expensive items that are at risk of damage or loss. This may include renter's insurance, car insurance, or health insurance, which can help you cover unexpected expenses related to these areas.

By managing healthcare expenses and unexpected expenses effectively, college students can reduce their financial stress and achieve their financial goals more quickly. The key is to stay informed, create a plan for managing your expenses, and take action to reduce your expenses and increase your income. By doing so, you can achieve financial security and independence, reduce financial stress, and achieve your financial aspirations.

J. Maximizing income

Maximizing income is an important part of personal finance for college students, particularly if you are working part-time or pursuing a side hustle. Increasing your income can help you achieve your financial goals more quickly and reduce financial stress.

To maximize your income, you should start by exploring your options for earning additional income, whether it's through part-time work, freelancing, or starting your own business. You should also look for ways to increase your income in your current job or field of study, such as through internships or job promotions.

Here are some strategies for maximizing income:

Pursue part-time work

Pursuing part-time work is a good option for maximizing income, particularly if you have a flexible schedule or are willing to work evenings or weekends. Part-time work can include a variety of options, such as retail, hospitality, or office work.

Explore freelance or contract work

Freelance or contract work can be a good option for maximizing income, particularly if you have a specialized skill set or expertise in a particular area. Freelance work can include a variety of options, such as writing, graphic design, or web development.

Start a side hustle

Starting a side hustle is another way to maximize income, particularly if you have an entrepreneurial spirit or are passionate about a particular project or product. Side hustles can include a variety of options, such as starting a blog, selling handmade items, or offering a service such as tutoring or pet-sitting.

K. Investing for the future

Investing for the future is an important part of personal finance for college students, particularly if you are interested in building wealth and achieving long-term financial goals. Investing can help you grow your money over time, potentially generating passive income and providing a source of financial security in the future.

To start investing, you should start by exploring your options for investing, whether it's through stocks, mutual funds, real estate, or other investment vehicles. You should also take into account your risk tolerance, investment goals, and time horizon.

Here are some strategies for investing for the future:

Start small

Starting small is a good option for investing, particularly if you are new to investing or have a limited budget. You can start by investing in a low-cost index fund or mutual fund, which can provide a diversified portfolio of stocks and bonds.

Explore your options

Exploring your options for investing is important, particularly if you have a particular interest or expertise in a certain area. This may include exploring real estate investments, investing in a particular industry or sector, or investing in socially responsible funds.

Seek professional advice

Seeking professional advice is another way to invest for the future, particularly if you are new to investing or have a complex financial situation. A financial advisor can help you identify your investment goals, manage your portfolio, and provide guidance on investment strategies.

By maximizing income and investing for the future, college students can achieve their financial goals and build a solid foundation for financial security and independence. The key is to stay informed, take action, and be proactive in managing your personal finances. By doing so, you can achieve financial security and independence, reduce financial stress, and achieve your financial aspirations.

Conclusion

Personal finance can be a daunting topic for college students, but it is an essential skill that can provide a solid foundation for financial security and independence. By understanding basic financial terms and concepts, setting financial goals, creating a budget, and managing income and expenses effectively, college students can reduce their financial stress and achieve their financial goals more quickly.

In addition, by maximizing income and investing for the future, college students can build long-term financial security and achieve their financial aspirations. The key is to stay informed, take action, and be proactive in managing your personal finances.

While personal finance may seem overwhelming, it's important to remember that it's a journey, not a destination. By taking small steps and making gradual improvements to your financial habits, you can achieve financial security and independence over time. With the right mindset, knowledge, and tools, you can take control of your finances and achieve your financial aspirations.

5

GETTING A SAVINGS AND TURNING IT INTO INVESTMENTS

Saving is an essential component of personal finance for college students, and it is crucial to start early and remain consistent. By saving, you can establish an emergency fund, save for a down payment on a house, or invest for the future. By starting to save early and consistently, you can create a solid financial foundation that can help you achieve your financial goals.

Here are some strategies for saving:

Start small: Starting small is a good option for saving, particularly if you are new to saving or have a limited budget. You can begin by setting aside a small amount each month and gradually increasing your savings over time.

For instance, if you save $10 per week, you will have saved $520 at the end of the year. This may not seem like a significant amount, but over time, it will add up.

Use automatic savings: Using automatic savings is another way to save effectively, particularly if you have trouble sticking to a savings plan. You can set up automatic transfers from your checking account to a savings account, making it easier to save consistently over time.

For instance, you can set up an automatic transfer of $25 from your checking account to your savings account every month. By the end of the year, you will have saved $300 without even thinking about it.

Reduce expenses: Reducing your expenses is another way to save effectively, particularly if you are on a limited budget. This may include finding ways to save on housing, transportation, food, and other areas of your budget.

For instance, you can save on food expenses by cooking your meals at home instead of eating out. This can help you save money and improve your health at the same time.

Investing is another important aspect of personal finance for college students. Investing can help you grow your money over time, potentially generating passive income and providing a source of financial security in the future.

Here are some types of investment options available:

Stocks: Stocks are a type of investment that involves buying ownership in a company. Stocks can provide potential for high returns but also come with risks, as the value of stocks can fluctuate based on market conditions.

For instance, if you invest in a stock that grows by 10% in a year, you will earn $10 for every $100 you invest.

Bonds: Bonds are a type of investment that involves lending money to a company or government entity. Bonds provide a more stable investment option than stocks but typically offer lower returns.

For instance, if you invest in a bond that pays a 3% annual interest rate, you will earn $3 for every $100 you invest.

Mutual funds: Mutual funds are a type of investment that involves pooling money with other investors to buy a diversified portfolio of stocks and bonds. Mutual funds offer a convenient way to invest in a diversified portfolio, but typically come with fees and expenses.

For instance, if you invest in a mutual fund that has an expense ratio of 1%, you will pay $1 in fees for every $100 you invest.

Developing an investment strategy is an important aspect of personal finance for college students. An investment strategy can help you identify your investment goals, manage your portfolio, and make informed investment decisions over time.

Here are some strategies for developing an investment strategy:

Identify your investment goals: Identifying your investment goals is the first step in developing an investment strategy. This may include identifying your risk tolerance, investment horizon, and financial aspirations.

For instance, if your investment goal is to save for a down payment on a house in five years, you will need to choose investments that are less risky than those you might choose for a long-term retirement goal.

Choose a diversified portfolio: Choosing a diversified portfolio can help you manage risk and achieve a balance between risk and return. This may involve investing in a mix of stocks, bonds, and other asset classes, depending on your risk tolerance and investment goals.

For instance, if you have a high risk tolerance and a long investment horizon, you might consider investing in a mix of domestic and international stocks. On the other hand, if you have a low risk tolerance and a short investment horizon, you might consider investing in bonds and other fixed-income investments.

Monitor your portfolio: Monitoring your portfolio regularly is important to ensure that it remains in line with your investment goals and risk tolerance. This may involve re-balancing your portfolio periodically to maintain a target asset allocation.

For instance, if your target asset allocation is 70% stocks and 30% bonds, you may need to re-balance your portfolio periodically to maintain this balance as market conditions change.

Minimize investment fees and expenses: Minimizing investment fees and expenses is another important aspect of developing an effective investment strategy. This may involve choosing low-cost investments, avoiding frequent trading, and considering tax implications when making investment decisions.

For instance, if you invest in a mutual fund that charges a 1% annual expense ratio, you will pay $1 in fees for every $100 you invest. Over time, these fees can add up and eat into your investment returns.

Another important aspect of saving and investing for college students is the power of compounding. Compounding is the process by which your money earns interest, and then that interest earns interest, creating a snowball effect of growth over time.

Here are some strategies for taking advantage of the power of compounding:

Start saving early: Starting to save early is one of the most effective ways to take advantage of compounding. By starting to save early and consistently, you can maximize the amount of time your money has to grow through compounding.

For instance, if you start saving $100 per month at age 25 and earn an average annual return of 7%, you will have saved over $100,000 by age 50.

Take advantage of tax-advantaged accounts: Tax-advantaged accounts, such as IRAs and 401(k) plans, allow your money to grow tax-free or tax-deferred, maximizing the power of compounding.

For instance, if you invest $5,000 per year in an IRA starting at age 25 and earn an average annual return of 7%, you will have saved over $1 million by age 65.

Reinvest your earnings: Reinvesting your earnings back into your portfolio can help you take advantage of compounding over time. This may involve reinvesting dividends and interest, rather than taking them as cash.

For instance, if you reinvest your dividends and interest for 20 years and earn an average annual return of 7%, your portfolio will grow by over 250%.

Stay invested for the long-term: Staying invested for the long-term is another important aspect of taking advantage of compounding. By avoiding emotional investment decisions and staying invested over the long-term, you can maximize the power of compounding.

For instance, if you invest $10,000 in the S&P 500 index at age 25 and stay invested for 40 years, your investment will grow to over $250,000, assuming an average annual return of 7%.

By understanding the power of compounding and implementing strategies to take advantage of it, college students can achieve long-term financial growth and security.

Managing risk is another important aspect of saving and investing for college students. Risk management involves identifying and assessing risks, and taking steps to reduce or mitigate those risks.

Here are some strategies for managing risk when saving and investing:

Diversify your portfolio: Diversifying your portfolio by investing in a mix of asset classes can help reduce the risk of loss due to market fluctuations. For instance, you might invest in a mix of stocks, bonds, and cash.

Avoid market timing: Trying to time the market can be a risky strategy that can lead to missed opportunities and losses. Instead of trying to time the market, focus on building a diversified portfolio that can help you weather market fluctuations.

Have a long-term investment horizon: Having a long-term investment horizon can help reduce the impact of short-term market fluctuations. By staying invested for the long-term, you can take advantage of compounding and achieve greater financial growth over time.

Set realistic expectations: Setting realistic expectations for investment returns can help you avoid making emotional investment decisions and taking on too much risk. By understanding the risks and potential rewards of different types of investments, you can make informed investment decisions that align with your goals and risk tolerance.

Use stop-loss orders: Stop-loss orders can be used to automatically sell an investment if it reaches a certain price, helping to limit losses. For instance, you might set a stop-loss order on a stock you own that will automatically sell the stock if it falls below a certain price.

By understanding risk management and implementing strategies to mitigate risk when saving and investing, college students can achieve long-term financial growth and security.

Asset allocation is the process of dividing your portfolio among different types of assets, such as stocks, bonds, and cash, to achieve a balance between risk and return.

Here are some strategies for implementing effective asset allocation:

Identify your risk tolerance: Understanding your risk tolerance is the first step in implementing an effective asset allocation strategy. Your risk tolerance will depend on a variety of factors, including your age, investment goals, and financial situation.

Choose a target asset allocation: Choosing a target asset allocation involves identifying the percentage of your portfolio you want to allocate to different types of assets, based on your risk tolerance and investment goals. For instance, you might choose to allocate 60% of your portfolio to stocks and 40% to bonds.

Monitor your portfolio: Monitoring your portfolio regularly is important to ensure that your actual asset allocation remains in line with your target allocation. This may involve re-balancing your portfolio periodically to maintain your target allocation.

Rebalance your portfolio: Rebalancing your portfolio involves buying and selling investments to bring your actual asset allocation back in line with your target allocation. For instance, if your target asset allocation is 60% stocks and 40% bonds, you might need to sell some of your stocks and buy more bonds to rebalance your portfolio.

By implementing an effective asset allocation strategy, college students can achieve a balance between risk and return, reduce the impact of market fluctuations, and achieve long-term financial growth and security.

Fees and expenses can eat away at your investment returns over time, so it's important to understand these costs and choose investments with low fees and expenses whenever possible.

Here are some strategies for reducing investment fees and expenses:

Choose low-cost investments: Choosing low-cost investments, such as index funds, can help reduce the impact of fees and expenses on your investment returns.

Avoid frequent trading: Frequent trading can lead to higher fees and expenses, so it's important to avoid this practice whenever possible.

Consider tax implications: Taxes can also impact your investment returns, so it's important to consider tax implications when making investment decisions.

For instance, if you invest in a mutual fund with a high turnover rate, you may be subject to capital gains taxes, which can eat away at your investment returns.

Be aware of hidden fees: Some investments may have hidden fees and expenses that are not immediately apparent, such as administrative fees and account maintenance fees. It's important to read the fine print and be aware of these fees before investing.

By understanding the impact of fees and expenses on investment returns and implementing strategies to reduce these costs, college students can maximize their investment returns over the long-term.

Evaluating investment opportunities is an important aspect of investing for college students. It involves researching different types of investments and assessing their potential risks and rewards.

Here are some strategies for evaluating investment opportunities:

Research the investment: Researching the investment is an important first step in evaluating its potential risks and rewards. This may involve reading financial reports, analyzing market trends, and researching the company or fund offering the investment.

Consider the potential risks and rewards: Assessing the potential risks and rewards of an investment involves looking at factors such as the investment's past performance, the market it operates in, and any potential regulatory or legal risks.

Evaluate the investment's fit with your goals and risk tolerance: Evaluating whether an investment is a good fit with your investment goals and risk tolerance is an important aspect of making informed investment decisions.

Seek professional advice: Seeking professional advice from a financial advisor or investment professional can help you make informed investment decisions and avoid costly mistakes.

By understanding how to evaluate investment opportunities and making informed investment decisions, college students can achieve long-term financial growth and security.

Conclusion

Saving and investing for college students is an important aspect of achieving long-term financial growth and security. By understanding the basics of personal finance, managing income and expenses, and developing an effective investment strategy, college students can achieve their financial goals and build a strong financial foundation for the future.

While the process of saving and investing can seem daunting at first, taking small steps and being consistent can lead to big results over time. By starting early, taking advantage of the power of compounding, and minimizing fees and expenses, college students can achieve long-term financial growth and security, regardless of their current financial situation.

6

TAKING CONTROL OF DEBT

Managing debt is an essential part of achieving financial freedom and security. College students are often faced with significant debt from student loans, credit cards, and other sources, making it essential to develop a plan for managing and reducing debt. In this chapter, we'll explore various strategies for managing debt, including understanding the different types of debt, creating a plan for paying off debt, and implementing strategies for avoiding and reducing debt.

A. Understanding Different Types of Debt

Understanding the different types of debt is the first step in managing debt effectively. There are several types of debt that college students may encounter, including:

Student loan debt: Student loan debt is one of the most common types of debt for college students. It's essential to understand the different types of student loans, including federal and private loans, and to explore options for managing student loan debt, such as income-driven repayment plans and loan forgiveness programs.

Credit card debt: Credit card debt is another common type of debt for college students. It's important to understand how credit cards work, including interest rates, fees, and rewards programs, and to develop a plan for managing credit card debt, such as paying off balances in full each month.

Medical debt: Medical debt can be a significant burden for college students, especially those who are uninsured or underinsured. It's important to understand the options for managing medical debt, including negotiating bills and seeking financial assistance.

Tax debt: Tax debt can be a significant burden for college students, especially those who have not properly managed their tax withholding or have self-employment income. Understanding options for managing tax debt, such as payment plans, can help you avoid serious consequences like wage garnishment, liens on your property, and damage to your credit score.

Payday loans: Payday loans can be a tempting option for those who need quick cash, but they often come with high-interest rates and fees that can make them difficult to repay. It's important to understand the costs of payday loans, create a plan for repayment, and explore alternative sources of credit.

Understanding the different types of debt is an important step in managing debt effectively. Each type of debt has its unique features and requires a tailored approach for managing it effectively.

B. Creating a Plan for Managing and Paying off Debt

Once you understand the different types of debt, the next step is to create a plan for managing and paying off debt. Here are some strategies for managing and paying off debt:

Prioritize your debt: Prioritizing your debt is an essential step in managing debt effectively. Consider paying off debt with the highest interest rates first to minimize the total cost of your debt over time.

Consider debt consolidation: Debt consolidation can help you streamline your debt payments and reduce your overall interest rate.

There are several options for debt consolidation, including balance transfer credit cards, personal loans, and home equity loans.

Create a budget: Creating a budget can help you manage your debt by providing a clear picture of your income and expenses. Use your budget to identify areas where you can reduce your expenses and free up money for debt repayment.

Consider debt settlement: Debt settlement involves negotiating with your creditors to settle your debt for less than the total amount owed. It's important to note that debt settlement can negatively impact your credit score and there's no guarantee that your creditors will agree to the settlement.

C. Strategies for Avoiding and Reducing Debt

In addition to managing and paying off debt, it's important to implement strategies for avoiding and reducing debt. Here are some strategies for avoiding and reducing debt:

Live below your means: Living below your means can help you avoid taking on more debt than you can afford. By keeping your expenses lower than your income, you can avoid taking on debt and free up money for debt repayment.

Build an emergency fund: Building an emergency fund can help you avoid taking on debt in the event of an unexpected expense or loss of income. Aim to save at least three to six months' worth of living expenses in an emergency fund.

Avoid unnecessary purchases: Avoiding unnecessary purchases can help you free up money for debt repayment and avoid taking on more debt. Before making a purchase, ask yourself if it's something you really need and if you can afford it.

Use credit cards responsibly: Using credit cards responsibly can help you avoid accumulating credit card debt. Only use credit cards for purchases you can afford to pay off in full each month, and always pay your bills on time to avoid late fees and interest charges.

Understanding the impact of interest rates is also crucial for managing debt effectively. Interest rates can have a significant impact on the total cost of your debt over time. For example, a loan with a high-interest rate can result in significantly higher total interest costs than a loan with a lower interest rate. Understanding the impact of interest rates can help college students make informed decisions about taking on new debt and prioritizing debt repayment.

Another important topic to cover is refinancing debt. Refinancing debt, such as through a student loan refinance or mortgage refinance, can help reduce your interest rates and make your debt more manageable. However, it's important to carefully consider the costs and benefits of refinancing before making a decision.

Dealing with debt collectors can be intimidating and stressful, but it's important to understand your rights and obligations under the law. Knowing your rights can help you navigate the debt collection process and avoid being taken advantage of.

One more topic that could be included in the section on managing debt is dealing with student loan debt. Student loan debt can be a significant burden for college students, and it's important to have a plan for managing this type of debt. Understanding your repayment options, considering loan forgiveness programs, refinancing your loans, and seeking professional advice can help you manage your student loan debt effectively.

Managing medical debt is another important topic to cover in this chapter. Medical debt is a common type of debt that can be challenging to manage, especially for those who are uninsured or underinsured. Negotiating your bills, seeking financial assistance, and considering payment plans can help you manage your medical debt effectively.

Understanding debt-to-income ratios is also important. Debt-to-income ratios are an important measure of your financial health and can be used by lenders to assess your ability to repay debt. Understanding your debt-to-income ratio can help you make informed decisions about taking on new debt and managing your existing debt.

Managing and preventing identity theft is another important topic to cover in this chapter. Identity theft is a growing problem and can lead to the accumulation of significant amounts of debt in your name. By taking steps to manage and prevent identity theft, college students can protect themselves from the negative financial impacts of this crime.

In conclusion, managing debt is an essential part of achieving financial freedom and security. College students must understand the different types of debt, create a plan for managing and paying off debt, and implement strategies for avoiding and reducing debt. By understanding the impact of interest rates, refinancing debt, dealing with debt collectors, and managing medical debt, college students can achieve greater financial freedom and security. Additionally, understanding debt-to-income ratios, managing and preventing identity theft, dealing with tax debt, and avoiding and managing payday loans can help college students manage debt effectively and achieve their financial goals.

7

UNDERSTANDING WHAT THE FUTURE HOLDS

Planning for the future is an essential part of personal finance, and college students can benefit greatly from developing a comprehensive plan. Here are some key topics to consider when planning for the future:

Funding education: Paying for education can be a significant expense, but there are several ways to fund education, including scholarships, grants, student loans, and work-study programs. By understanding your options and developing a plan for funding your education, you can achieve your educational goals without incurring too much debt.

Emergency fund: An emergency fund is a critical part of a long-term financial plan. It is a reserve of money set aside for unexpected expenses such as medical bills, car repairs, or job loss. Having an emergency fund can help you avoid taking on debt and maintain financial stability during challenging times.

Estate planning: Estate planning involves making decisions about your assets, including your money, property, and other valuable possessions. It is important to create an estate plan to ensure that your assets are distributed according to your wishes after your death.

Insurance: Insurance is an essential part of a long-term financial plan. It helps protect you and your assets from unexpected events such as accidents, illness, and natural disasters. There are several types of insurance, including health insurance, life insurance, and homeowner's insurance.

Retirement planning: Retirement planning is an important part of a long-term financial plan. It involves saving and investing money to provide for your future needs and expenses when you are no longer working. There are several retirement planning options available, including individual retirement accounts (IRAs), employer-sponsored retirement plans, and Social Security.

Tax planning: Tax planning involves making strategic decisions about your finances to minimize your tax liability. This can involve taking advantage of deductions and credits, making contributions to tax-advantaged accounts, and structuring your finances in a tax-efficient manner.

Investment planning: Investment planning involves making decisions about how to invest your money to achieve your financial goals. There are several investment options available, including stocks, bonds, mutual funds, and real estate. It's important to understand the risks and potential rewards associated with each investment option.

Charitable giving: Charitable giving is the act of donating money or other resources to a charitable organization or cause. Many college students may not have a lot of money to donate, but even small contributions can make a big impact. Charitable giving can help you feel good about making a difference in the world while also providing potential tax benefits.

By understanding these topics and others, college students can gain a more comprehensive understanding of planning for the future and achieve greater financial freedom and security. Let's take a closer look at each of these topics.

Funding Education:

Education is one of the biggest expenses that college students will face. However, there are several ways to fund your education without going into significant debt. Scholarships and grants are a great way to get free money for college. Many colleges and universities offer scholarships and grants based on academic achievement, athletic ability, and other criteria. You can also look for scholarships and grants from private organizations and businesses.

If you do need to take out student loans, make sure to do your research and understand the terms and conditions of the loans. Federal student loans typically offer lower interest rates and more flexible repayment options than private student loans. Work-study programs are another option to consider, as they allow you to earn money while attending school.

Emergency Fund:

An emergency fund is a critical part of a long-term financial plan. It is important to have a reserve of money set aside for unexpected expenses such as medical bills, car repairs, or job loss. Experts recommend having three to six months' worth of living expenses saved in an emergency fund.

To start building your emergency fund, set aside a small amount of In addition to the above strategies, it's important for college students to understand the consequences of unpaid debt. Unpaid debt can lead to serious consequences, such as damage to credit scores, legal action, and wage garnishment. These consequences can have long-term impacts on financial stability, making it more difficult to secure loans, find employment, and achieve other financial goals.

Another important consideration for managing debt is dealing with debt collectors. It's important for college students to understand their rights and obligations under the law when dealing with debt collectors. While debt collection can be intimidating and stressful, knowing your rights can help you navigate the process and avoid being taken advantage of.

In addition to these topics, there are several other strategies and considerations that can help college students effectively manage debt, including:

Understanding the impact of interest rates: Interest rates can have a significant impact on the total cost of debt over time. By understanding how interest rates can affect debt, college students can make informed decisions about taking on new debt and prioritizing debt repayment.

Refinancing debt: Refinancing debt, such as through a student loan refinance or mortgage refinance, can help reduce interest rates and make debt more manageable. However, it's important to carefully consider the costs and benefits of refinancing before making a decision.

Dealing with student loan debt: Student loan debt can be a significant burden for college students, and it's important to have a plan for managing this type of debt. Strategies for dealing with student loan debt include understanding repayment options, considering loan forgiveness programs, and seeking professional advice.

Managing medical debt: Medical debt is a common type of debt that can be challenging to manage, especially for those who are uninsured or underinsured. Strategies for managing medical debt include negotiating bills, seeking financial assistance, and considering payment plans.

Understanding debt-to-income ratios: Debt-to-income ratios are an important measure of financial health and can be used by lenders to assess the ability to repay debt. Understanding debt-to-income ratios can help college students make informed decisions about taking on new debt and managing existing debt.

Managing and preventing identity theft: Identity theft is a growing problem and can lead to the accumulation of significant amounts of debt in one's name. By taking steps to manage and prevent identity theft, college students can protect themselves from the negative financial impacts of this crime.

Dealing with tax debt: Tax debt can be a significant burden for college students, especially if they have not properly managed their tax withholding or have self-employment income. Strategies for managing tax debt include understanding payment plan options, seeking professional advice, and understanding the consequences of unpaid tax debt.

Avoiding and managing payday loans: Payday loans can be a tempting option for those who need quick cash, but they often come with high interest rates and fees that can make them difficult to repay. Strategies for avoiding and managing payday loans include considering alternative sources of credit, understanding the costs involved, and creating a plan for repayment.

By including these topics and strategies, college students can gain a more comprehensive understanding of managing debt and achieving greater financial freedom and security. While managing debt can be challenging, with the right strategies and knowledge, college students can take control of their finances and achieve their financial goals. In addition to understanding the importance of saving and investing, college students also need to know about the risks and potential rewards of different investment options. Here are some important investment strategies to consider:

Stocks: Stocks are shares of ownership in a company and can potentially provide significant returns over the long term. However, they are also subject to market volatility and can be risky, especially for those who are new to investing. It's important to do your research and understand the company's financial health and performance before investing in their stock.

Bonds: Bonds are a type of debt investment where you lend money to a company or government and receive interest payments over time. Bonds are generally considered to be less risky than stocks, but also typically provide lower returns.

Mutual funds: Mutual funds are a type of investment where you pool your money with other investors to purchase a diversified portfolio of stocks, bonds, and other securities. This can provide a more diversified investment portfolio, which can help reduce risk.

Exchange-traded funds (ETFs): ETFs are similar to mutual funds, but they are traded on the stock exchange like a stock. This can provide more flexibility and liquidity than traditional mutual funds.

Real estate: Real estate can be a good long-term investment, but it can also be risky and require a significant upfront investment. College students may want to consider investing in real estate through a real estate investment trust (REIT), which allows you to invest in real estate without owning physical property.

It's important to remember that all investments come with risks, and it's important to do your research and understand the potential risks and rewards of each investment option. Seeking the advice of a financial advisor or investment professional can also be helpful in making informed investment decisions.

By developing an investment strategy and understanding the potential risks and rewards of different investment options, college students can achieve greater financial security and build wealth over time. It's important for college students to remember that investing is a long-term strategy and requires patience and discipline. Here are some additional tips for developing a successful investment strategy:

Set clear investment goals: Before you start investing, it's important to set clear goals for what you want to achieve. This can help you stay focused and avoid making impulsive investment decisions.

Diversify your portfolio: Diversifying your portfolio can help reduce risk and protect your investments from market volatility. This means investing in a mix of different asset classes, such as stocks, bonds, and real estate.

Rebalance your portfolio regularly: As your investments grow and change over time, it's important to periodically rebalance your portfolio to ensure that it remains aligned with your investment goals.

Avoid high-risk investments: While high-risk investments may offer the potential for high returns, they also come with a greater potential for loss. College students should focus on building a diversified, low-risk investment portfolio to achieve long-term financial security.

Consider the impact of taxes: Taxes can significantly impact your investment returns, so it's important to consider the tax implications of your investment decisions.

Be patient and disciplined: Successful investing requires patience and discipline, and it's important to avoid making impulsive investment decisions based on short-term market fluctuations.

By following these tips and developing a disciplined investment strategy, college students can achieve long-term financial security and build wealth over time.

Finally, it's important to remember that investing is just one part of a larger financial plan. College students should also focus on managing their income, expenses, debt, and savings to achieve greater financial security and build a strong foundation for their future. By following the advice in this book, college students can gain the knowledge and tools they need to achieve financial success and build a bright future.

8

REAL WORLD CONSIDERATIONS

A. Navigating financial challenges in the real world

After college, young adults will face many new financial challenges, such as renting an apartment, buying a car, and managing bills. These challenges can seem overwhelming, but with the right knowledge and strategies, they can be navigated successfully.

One important step in navigating financial challenges is to create a realistic budget that accounts for all of your expenses and income. It's also important to understand how to manage debt, including credit card debt and student loan debt. This can involve creating a plan for repayment, negotiating with lenders, and exploring options for refinancing.

Another important aspect of navigating financial challenges is to understand the value of emergency savings. Building an emergency fund can help protect you from unexpected expenses, such as car repairs or medical bills, and can help you avoid taking on additional debt.

B. Strategies for building credit and managing credit scores

Building good credit is an important part of achieving financial security and can help you access better rates on loans and credit cards. Here are some strategies for building credit and managing credit scores:

Make on-time payments: Paying your bills on time is one of the most important factors in building good credit. Set up automatic payments or create a reminder system to help you stay on track.

Keep your credit utilization low: Your credit utilization, or the amount of credit you're using compared to your total credit limit, can impact your credit score. Try to keep your credit utilization below 30% to maintain a good credit score.

Monitor your credit report: Your credit report is a record of your credit history and can impact your credit score. Review your credit report regularly and dispute any errors or inaccuracies.

Consider a secured credit card: If you have little or no credit history, a secured credit card can be a good way to build credit. A secured credit card requires a deposit, which serves as your credit limit.

C. Making smart financial decisions as a young adult

As a young adult, you will be faced with many financial decisions, such as choosing a job, renting an apartment, and investing in your future. Here are some strategies for making smart financial decisions:

Set financial goals: Setting specific financial goals, such as saving for a down payment on a home or paying off student loan debt, can help you stay focused and motivated.

Research your options: Before making a major financial decision, such as choosing a job or buying a car, it's important to do your research and compare your options. This can help you make an informed decision that aligns with your financial goals.

Seek professional advice: When making complex financial decisions, such as investing in the stock market or starting a business, it can be helpful to seek advice from a financial professional or mentor. They can provide guidance and help you make informed decisions.

Continuously learn about personal finance: Personal finance is a complex and ever-changing field, and it's important to stay up-to-date on the latest trends and strategies. Reading books, attending seminars, and following personal finance blogs can help you stay informed and make smart financial decisions.

D. Additional Topics

Understanding the cost of living: For young adults, understanding the cost of living in different areas can help them make informed decisions about where to live and work after graduation. For example, if a college graduate is offered a job in a new city, it's important to evaluate the cost of living in that city to determine if the salary offered will cover their expenses.

Navigating job benefits: Job benefits, such as healthcare and retirement plans, can have a significant impact on a young adult's financial health

Navigating financial independence: As college students transition into the working world and begin to support themselves financially, it's important to understand the various financial decisions that come with independence. Here are some strategies for navigating financial independence:

Establish an emergency fund: An emergency fund can help you prepare for unexpected expenses and provide a financial safety net.

Create a plan for saving and investing: As you begin to earn income, it's important to create a plan for saving and investing that aligns with your financial goals and values.

Understand and manage your credit: Maintaining good credit is important for accessing credit and loans in the future, so it's important to understand how to manage your credit and improve your credit score.

Learn how to negotiate: Negotiation is an important skill for navigating various financial situations, such as salary negotiations and purchasing a car or home.

To further illustrate these points, here are a few examples:

When it comes to establishing an emergency fund, consider setting aside three to six months' worth of living expenses in a savings account. This can help you weather unexpected financial challenges, such as a job loss or medical emergency, without having to rely on credit cards or loans.

Creating a plan for saving and investing can also help you achieve your long-term financial goals, such as buying a home or retiring comfortably. For example, you might consider contributing to a 401(k) or individual retirement account (IRA) to save for retirement, or investing in a low-cost index fund to build wealth over time.

Understanding and managing your credit is also important for achieving financial independence. This might involve monitoring your credit score regularly, paying your bills on time, and avoiding carrying high levels of credit card debt. By maintaining good credit, you can access credit and loans at lower interest rates, which can save you money over time.

Finally, learning how to negotiate can help you make the most of your money in a variety of situations. For example, when negotiating your salary, it's important to research salary ranges for similar positions and prepare a persuasive argument for why you deserve a higher salary. When purchasing a car, negotiating the price and terms of the loan can also help you save money over the long term.

By applying these strategies and others, college students can navigate the complex financial landscape of the real world and build a secure financial future for themselves.

9

FINAL THOUGHTS

Congratulations on completing this guide to personal finance for college students! By now, you should have a comprehensive understanding of the essential concepts and strategies for managing your finances, building wealth, and achieving financial independence.

In this book, we covered a wide range of topics, from setting financial goals and creating a budget to managing debt, saving and investing, and navigating real-world financial situations. We explored the importance of establishing good financial habits early in life, and the benefits of making informed financial decisions that can help you achieve your long-term goals.

Throughout this book, we emphasized the importance of taking a proactive approach to managing your finances. This involves developing a comprehensive understanding of your financial situation, setting clear goals and creating a plan to achieve them, and taking action to make informed decisions that can help you build a secure financial future.

While the world of personal finance can be complex and overwhelming, we hope that this guide has provided you with the tools and knowledge you need to navigate this landscape with confidence. Whether you are looking to save for a down payment on a home, pay off student loans, or simply build a more secure financial future for yourself, the principles and strategies we have discussed in this book can help you get there.

As you continue on your financial journey, there are a few key takeaways that we want to emphasize:

Start early: The earlier you begin developing good financial habits, the more time you have to benefit from their effects. Whether you are just starting college or are already in the workforce, it's never too early to begin thinking about your financial future.

Set clear goals: Without clear financial goals, it can be difficult to know where to focus your energy and resources. Take the time to think about what you want to achieve in the short and long term, and create a plan to get there.

Be proactive: Managing your finances requires ongoing effort and attention. Rather than simply reacting to financial challenges as they arise, take a proactive approach to building wealth and managing debt.

Educate yourself: The more you know about personal finance, the better equipped you will be to make informed financial decisions. Take advantage of the resources available to you, including books, websites, financial advisors, and other professionals.

Stay disciplined: Building wealth and achieving financial independence requires discipline and perseverance. Stay focused on your goals, and don't be afraid to make sacrifices in the short term to achieve long-term success.

By following these principles and putting the strategies we have discussed into action, you can build a secure financial future for yourself and achieve your financial goals. Remember that personal finance is a lifelong journey, and that there will be ups and downs along the way. But with determination, discipline, and the knowledge you have gained from this book, you can navigate the complex world of personal finance with confidence and success.

We hope that you have found this guide to be informative and helpful, and we wish you the best of luck on your financial journey. May you enjoy a life of financial freedom and security!

It's important to remember that personal finance is a lifelong journey. As a college student, you have the opportunity to establish good habits and make informed decisions that will set you on the path to financial success. The principles and strategies outlined in this book can serve as a foundation for your financial future, but it's up to you to put them into practice and adapt them to your unique circumstances.

One of the most important things you can do as a young adult is to stay informed and educated about personal finance. Keep up with changes in the economy, tax laws, and financial products and services. Seek out resources and advice from reputable sources, such as financial advisors, consumer advocacy groups, and government agencies.

Another key to financial success is to maintain a growth mindset. Be open to learning, experimentation, and taking calculated risks. Recognize that setbacks and failures are a natural part of the process, and use them as opportunities to learn and grow.

Above all, remember that personal finance is about more than just money. It's about your values, priorities, and goals. By staying true to your values and priorities, setting clear goals, and making informed decisions, you can achieve greater financial freedom and security, and create a life of meaning and purpose.

In conclusion, I hope that this book has provided you with a solid foundation for understanding and managing your personal finances as a college student. By taking control of your finances and building good habits, you can create a more secure and fulfilling future. Remember, financial success is within your reach – all it takes is a little planning, discipline, and determination. Good luck on your journey!

Made in the USA
Monee, IL
04 November 2026

67376102R00039